MW01247235

Civil Rights Leaders

Contents

Susan B. Anthony thought that all Americans should have equal rights. In 1872, the law did not allow any women to vote. Anthony voted for President anyway.

Other women worked for suffrage, too.
Suffrage means "the right to vote." In 1920,
after Susan B. Anthony had died, a new law
finally gave women the right to vote.

Mary McLeod Bethune's parents had been slaves. Bethune believed that every black child should get an education. She started a school for girls in Florida.

Eleanor Roosevelt wanted to help others. She traveled all over the United States to find out what people needed. People called her "Rover" because she liked to "rove," or travel.

Mary McLeod Bethune and Eleanor Roosevelt worked together to help all American children get a good education. They also worked together at the United Nations.

In the early 1900s, baseball was segregated.
White people played in the major leagues.
Black people played in the Negro leagues.

Branch Rickey was president of the Brooklyn Dodgers. All the men playing on the Dodgers team were white. Mr. Rickey still wanted Jackie Robinson to play on the team.

Jackie Robinson joined the Dodgers. Many
people were mad to see a black person playing
on a white baseball team. Robinson was the
league's best new player that year.

In the South, black people had to sit at the back of the bus. Rosa Parks broke the law in Alabama. She would not move to the back of the bus to give a white man her seat.

Black people started a boycott. They all stopped riding the buses, and they walked or rode in cars together. They showed that they thought Rosa Parks was right.

Dr. Martin Luther King, Jr. wanted integration. Dr. King read about a man named Mohandas Gandhi. Gandhi helped his country become free without violence.

In August 1963, people marched in Washington, D.C. Thousands of people went to the Lincoln Memorial to say they wanted a better life for all Americans.

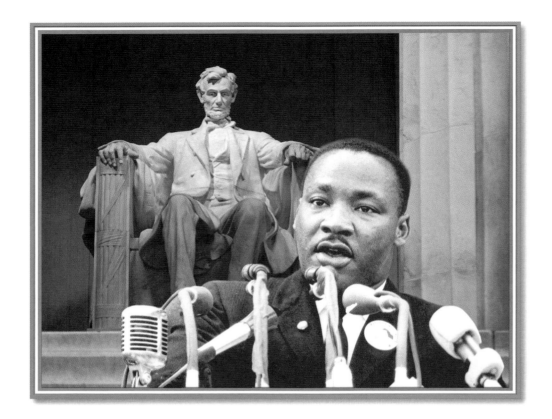

Dr. King spoke to all the people. He told about his dream of integration. In 1964, the U.S. government passed the Civil Rights Act, saying that segregation was wrong.

Migrant farmworkers move from place to place to find work. César Chávez grew up as a migrant farmworker. He and his family moved to a different farm almost every month.

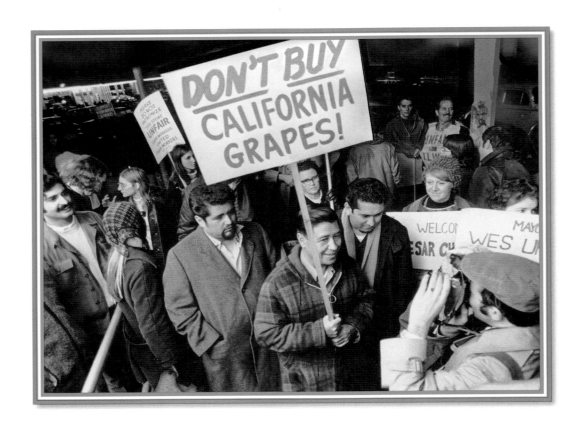

César Chávez wanted to help migrant workers make more money. He asked Americans not to buy grapes and lettuce. The boycott made farm owners pay more money to migrant workers.